I0345989

Beyond The Plain
E. Hughes

Copyright © 2024 E. Hughes

All rights reserved. No part of this book may be reproduced or transmitted in any form or by any means, electronic or mechanical, including photocopying, recording or by any information storage and retrieval system, without permission in writing from the publisher.

Love-LovePublishing—Madison, WI
PAPERBACK ISBN: 978-0-9973200-0-8
eBook ISBN: 978-1-961823-17-4
Library of Congress Control Number: 2018902028
Beyond the Plain / E. Hughes. Love-LovePublishing
Available formats: eBook
Paperback distribution

Third edition

Dedication

I dedicate this book to the voiceless and the "unloved."

You are loved.

I also dedicate this book to my wonderful husband Byron for his endless support, and my children Brandon, Bishop, AJ, and Blake, who inspire me every single day. I will forever be your mama bear.

I also dedicate this book to my late mother, Janice, who, despite her flaws, fears, and the challenges of loneliness, lived bravely to the very end. I pray for your eternal happiness and God's blessings.

INTRODUCTION

The poetry in *Beyond the Plain* was written over the span of many years, throughout my youth as a teen into early adulthood. During these formative years, poetry for me was not only a cathartic form of self-expression, but a matter of emotional survival. Most of the poems in this book use a rhyming scheme with a few that are in free verse. While the specter of sadness haunts the poetry in *Beyond the Plain*, glimmers hope and strength shines through in moments of despair.

Hang in there.

Other novels and works by E. Hughes:

Fiction:

Sixth Iteration
Disappear, Love
Business as Usual
Infatuation
A Mediterranean Romance: The Capa Royals
The Sapphire Chronicles: Broken Lair
Hello (A Screenplay)

Children's Books:

Penelope Helps Mom and Dad
Penelope: Be Kind to Animals
Penelope: Super Duper Spectacular Princess Ballerina
Penelope: Don't be afraid
Penelope Holiday Cheer
Kissing Henry (YA novel)

Nonfiction
Digital Smiles
Time and the Multi-Universe: A philosophy of time and time travel
Starting Your First Potted Vegetable Garden
Reality Unbound: The Digital Mind and the Nature of Reality

Contents

Dead Roses 1
One Breasted Woman 2
Nobody's Child 4
Lover's Clown 6
Evergreen 8
Beyond the Plain 10
And Dress Me as You Do... 12
A Snake Slid Under My Door 14
She Sat by the River 16
Melancholy 18
Young Mother's Lament 20
Life as a Dog 22
You're too Good For Me 25
Toxic Waste of the Human Soul 26
Optical Delusions of Life and Death 28
Whisper 30
Violins 31
Better Company 32
Too Dead to Die 34
I Too, Know of Rivers 36
Chimera of Light 38
Knowing is loving 39
Goodbye mommy 40
My Window of Hope 41
Something Wrong 42
Never Say Goodbye 44
Deceitful 45
Rest in Power 46
Child of the World 48

Beautiful 49
Never Born 50
Unable to Love 51
Black Woman's Blues 52
Just Biding My Time 54
I View the World from Swollen Eyes 55
Be Innocent Little One 57
Where I Want to Be 58
Moonstars 59
Listen 60
Sunrays 61
My Arrival 62
Loving Way 63
Make Love to Me 64
Come My Love 66
Friend 67
True Happiness 68
About the Author 70

Dead Roses

I can see my face in the gutter's mirror
reflecting my skin
now dry and withered.
My withered body lay dead in the street
my once praised beauty lies suffering in defeat.
Uprooted and discarded
I lay broken hearted
with my once fragrant skin
and limbs in the wind...

One Breasted Woman

A one breasted woman
sits in a field
with two babies between her thighs
she wonders which one she must kill
she looks into their eyes
her face clearly reveals
 the pain inside of her heart
 that I know she must feel
the sun bears down upon them
she curses him and asks,
"Why do you punish us so?"
As she aches in misery
of which of her children must go
drying her to the bone
the one breasted woman shivers
she loves him,
but the little one must go to the river.
The longest walk of their lives
the pits of their stomachs growl
as she waits
and she aches
the demise of her child
his large eyes narrow
he innocently smiles
so small and withered, floating away
down the still dusty river.
The women all look at each other
they know not what to say

as the one breasted woman
hobbles away.
Too weak to look back she lifts her apt breast
to feed her one child
she lays down to rest
in the distant dry field, a hollow drum beats
and though there is only one child left,
there is still,
not enough for the child to eat.
The one breasted woman releases a shiver.
Unable to cry,
 she returns to the river.

Nobody's child

She's never been mommy's little princess
neither daddy's little girl
left trapped underneath a rock
she was shown the dark side of the world.
But despite her torn skin and gritted teeth
she ambitiously crawls from beneath
this boulder somehow
with the aid of no one
she's nobody's child.
Though she seems unpleasant
stick around for a while
get to know her, she's nobody's child
you're bound to see her beautiful smile
though she often, wears a frown
living in a world where she doesn't belong
always singing her sad songs
of years, tears, of heartache and strife
living as she's lived, an ugly woman's life.
No one held her in their arms
no one protected her from harm
she is nobody, but flesh to feast
with no one's love to set her free
from the belly of the mountain, she'll climb
out somehow
from the depths of the ocean where she was
left to drown
don't cry for her, she's nobody's child.
Don't ever look into her deep brown eyes

no one sees the tears she cries
she is no one's wife, no one's sister
she's been gone for years, yet no one's
missed her.
She could use a friend, stick around for a while.
Love her or use her, she's nobody's child.

Lover's Clown

I wear my emotions like a badge of shame,
and my heartbreak like a crown,
I entertain his game, when his touches inflame,
my teardrops to make smiles out of frowns.
When I love him regardless,
even when he's heartless,
and laughs at my weary pain,
his touches inflame,
I wear my heartbreak like a crown,
I wear my emotions like a badge of shame,
for I am, my lover's clown.
I dangle from strings
of meaningless flings
and nothingness things
the shamefulness brings
when I dance to his song
he loves, and hugs
then leaves
I grieve
when he leaves me alone.
I beg him unsure
if I can endure
wearing the paint of jest.
The beating [of my heart] obscures
the feelings impure,
and the hollowing emptiness.
When sadness rings, the morning after
and the rising sun pulls me down

my tear drops bring forth his laughter
until my heartache halos me like a gleaming crown.
I wear my emotions like a badge of shame
for I am my lover's clown...

Evergreen

Ever green,
And evermore
seaweeds weaving
beyond the shore
where drops of sunshine
seems to pour
into Evergreen,
Forevermore.
A drop of moonlight
ocean waves
endless nights
Yield endless stars
For endless days
In the morn
The skies will blaze
In an amber, gold
and red-orange haze.
The evergreen will sway in the wind,
where streams move deftly,
and cobbled roads bend,
Where the sky and mountain,
melt into a blend,
beyond the horizon,
where clouds descend.
I stood beneath,
the evergreen,
my secret place,
near the ravine,

I rested in the moss,
Which kept me clean,
And drank from a fresh,
Mountain spring,
The sun broke through,
And down it beamed,
And cleansed my wretched soul serene,
Forevermore,
And evergreen.

Beyond The Plain

Walk with me
in the park
we'll hold hands
because it's dark
in our world
we're only two
there is me
and no one but you
the sky is glass
so we'll break through
and then we'll pass
beyond the blue...
Into twilight
where we will talk
amongst the stars
where we will walk.
Nothing will matter
but you and me
and we'll skip stars
over the sea
and build a tree house
on the moon
and shower ourselves
in the monsoon
and then we'll play
out in the rain
and roll down hills

beyond the plains.
We'll never say we love each other
let our actions be louder
than booming thunder
And then we'll bask
in the brooding light
and in the eve
we'll close our eyes
and I will die
come sun rise.
And I will bristle
at the rest
and I will nestle
into your chest
and you will hide
close to my breast.
Come run with me
out in the rain
down the hills
beyond the plains.

And Dress me as you do the Lilies in the Field

When the sun quietly rises, and night's chill splinters,
and my soul is as warm, as earth's molten center...
I lay still in my cocoon,
beholding its splendor.

But have you ever seen anything as beautiful
as a lily in a field?
or a willow tree blowing
at the top of a hill?

Just waiting on my slice
of that pie in the sky,
and when I'm suffering,
I ask Jesus why.

Lord dress me as you do,
the lilies in the field,
may my eyes sparkle like stars
and blaze like a shield.
Until...
I've seen anything as beautiful
as a shimmering lake,
as I lay still in my cocoon,
fully awake.

And when the Lord grants me a slice
of His pie in the sky
I'll make a pumpernickel road,

and bake in some rye.

My soul is warm
and energized with love,
a bridge to my Lord
and heaven thereof.

A snake slid under my door

I am awake at night,
to close my eyes no more,
in fear of the snake,
sliding,
underneath my door
begging me for,
its secrets to keep,
not to reveal its secrets,
 from my sleep,
about how he creeps,
 under my door to sweep,
my innocence,
from underneath my feet,
and rob me of my,
security.
I enter my room,
my bones a- shake,
in fear of, this slimy snake,
who will make,
me surely partake,
and violate,
my skin a- nake,
and have his cake, when violent.
I drag my feet,
and I dread
the snake that slides,
 into my bed,
behind my mother's oblivious head

and leaves me dead,
with nothing but,
the blood I shed,
and a tearful eye,
to peer the door within its sight,
with hate and fright,
awaiting daylight, that I long to see
to cast the snake,
as cast he be,
sliding,
 away with my innocence,
my innocence that he stole from me.

She Sat by the River

She sat by the river
her thin body listless, and hungered
she prays for a little rain to wet her tongue
in hopes of seeing
an old loved one. . .
Feeling too weak to cry
beneath the scorching sky
no swatting the buzzing flies
taunting, and dancing
and whizzing around her eyes.
She sat by the river
her mind gone
she sat by the river
no place to call home.
She sat by the river
looking for dad, or mama,
or ANYONE who
will come to her aid
in hopes the men won't come back
to invade,
With their machetes just like in the earlier raid
She fishes
and she fishes
while riding her boat
she misses the kisses
she sits by the river
where mama floats.
She sat by the river

and smelled rotting stink
she sat by the river
refusing to drink
she sat by the river
and watched mama sink
she sat by the river
her large eyes pink,
she died by the river
refusing to blink. . .

Melancholy

I doubt if anyone understands my frustration
my aggravation
my hesitation
to breathe...
the clean air
or if you have felt my despair
I doubt that you care...
so turn your backs on me
Life is a boulder
laid upon my shoulders
each year I grow 100 years older
and the world only grows colder...
Brutal
resistance is futile
free me, free me
these words are my tears
read them and weep
or prey on my fears
like lions upon sheep
I grow old
I grow weary
love is a theory
daring to be refuted
in a world where compassion is muted.
Turn your backs on me
After shedding rivers of blood
I forgot how to hug
my soul is a void

I doubt that you know I'm annoyed
or if you feel my despair
where I can smell
misery in the air...
my pain is to share
as these words are my tears
read them and weep
as I lay on railroad tracks...
pretending to sleep.

Young Mother's Lament

I have no husband
this I know
and got four children
who will grow
knowing me, but not their dad
I should be angry
but instead I'm glad.
This is the life
that I chose
it's a bed without the rose.
But must you look at me with such disdain?
It's not the path I've taken that causes me pain
it's hard enough without your stares
your judgment of me isn't fair
to scoff at my children with such glares
is too much for this young woman to bear
I know that I won't get to go to college
but doesn't mean I lack any knowledge
so spare me the unneeded sage
just because of my young age
stop treating me like I'm spoiled fruit
or as if I don't know my roots
and don't assume I'm some welfare fiend
or that I'll be a welfare queen
you'll never see my children unclean
so why must you treat me so mean?
I'm dying here doing the best that I can
don't look down at me because I have no man

do not pity me! Because you think I struggle
when you see the work, school, and family I juggle!
The scarlet letter isn't right!
I'm happy kissing their little foreheads at night
this is my life and I'm not changing still
it's you who make it hard to feel
keep your questions to yourself
we are happy, strong, and in good health
I didn't ask for your opinion,
I don't need you to forgive,
this is the life I want to live!
Yes it's hard, but we do not starve
and having a father for my children, I do not disregard
but sometimes it's just better this way
my beautiful children are here, and here to stay.
It's a bed without the rose,
don't look at me from down your nose.

Life as a Dog

Child, I'm sad cause I'm lonely and tired,
and can't keep up with my kids,
when they are wired.
And even though I'm young
I want to retire...
before I lay down
and just expire.

You might think I got no shame
because I took the time sit and complain.
And then you tell me to stop singing the blues
but would you be saying that if you were in my shoes?
You think you got problems?
Well I got the whole hog,
I tell you I live the life of a dog.

Workin' for just a little fee
can't even go on a shopping spree
can't never treat myself to nothin'
or take my kids out for ice cream or somethin',
I'm always mad cause I'm always broke,
can't even get my ego stroked,
and the last man I had, tried to choke
the livin' daylights out of me
when I asked to elope,
Can't even be somebody's wife,
You think you got problems?

Well I got strife
I tell you honey, it's a dog's life.

When I can't even pay my rent
and before I get it, my paycheck is spent
And then it's cold cause I ain't got no heat
and might as well be livin' on the street.
Well, you might think
I'm just another poor sap
cause you're enjoying life
and I'm living on scraps.
I'm not tryin' to make anybody feel guilt
for any success
they may have built
but a little compassion would be nice
and a lot less judgment
would suffice.
Cause you ain't that much better than me
just cause I live in poverty
you didn't do more than I did
cause your parents gave you more
than mine did.

I'm tired of tryin' and getting' nowhere,
and talkin' to people who don't even care
I'm tired of fighting to get ahead
sometimes I swear I'm better off dead!
I'm tired of worryin' about my bills
or if my son will get murdered or killed
or if some thug,
will hurt me too
I'm tired of feelin' so black and blue.

I'm tired of people being so damned callous
I'm tired of laws made out of malice
for poor folks
out of disdain
I'm tired of hatred and cold hard rain.

I'm sick and tired of pain and strife,
you might be living yours
but I'm livin' a dog's life.

Child I'm not tryin to make you feel pity
but try livin' life out in my city
try livin' life in my cold rain
try livin' life feelin' my pain
try livin' life feelin' my blues
try livin' life in my holey shoes
try livin' life on money from my bank
try livin' life driving on my empty tank
You think YOU got problems?
Well I got the WHOLE HOG,
try living your life, tired and dogged.

You're Too Good for Me

I know you will never love me,
so why get my hopes up high?
I know you will never love me,
so why do I try?
To tell you the truth,
I'm just not good enough for you,
what would you want with someone like me,
what can I really do?
You are so smart, vibrant, and successful,
you can have anyone you want,
you don't have to scream it in my face,
or stamp it on my heart.
I know I am just another warm body,
in your king sized bed.
I know I am not worthy of your love,
certainly not someone you would wed.
So I hang my head low,
don't look you in the eye,
I know you are too good for me,
so why do I even try?
When I see you with someone new,
I won't utter, not even a sound,
in fact I will bow out gracefully,
when you don't want me around.
I know you are too good for me,
because you are the best,
so I'll turn my empty palms away,
to give my heart a rest.

Toxic Waste of the Human Soul

Amazing though,
how we admire
those among us,
haughty and vain
whose power of audacity
we cannot expire
becomes a power,
we seek to attain

In a herd the fools will rush
and look for the weak
to taunt and crush
in a wake
of gravel and dust
break their spirit,
like links in a chain
stomp out their hearts
and vex their brains
Amazing how admired
are the haughty and vain
whom we cannot conquer
but seek to drain
to burn in our hearts
like lumps of coal
as toxic waste
for the human soul

Steady and long

have been the good
often strong
but misunderstood
a mild countenance
perceived as chaste
lacking in
toxic waste
not much for folly
for others to disgrace
faultless of greed
forbearing distaste

Blast the backs
of those in need
not compared to much
when stacked with good deeds
a master of self
seeks moderation
to shun those who seek
fame and adulation
and think the charitable
have been insane
for what is the purpose
if not for gain?

Amazing how admired,
are the haughty and vain
often arrogant
and truly inane
foul deeds
too many to name
whose power we seek
while drunk with shame.

Optical Delusions of Life and Death

I speak of souls and revolutions
annihilation of physical institution
fracture like light through a prism break
spiraling through space like a crystal plate
a beam refracting in magnetospheric violence
exploding into death with earth shattering silence!

Welcome to my truth
of non-existence
resist - my fleshly and metaphysical dichotomy
and rest on an axis of axenic spiritual reality.

You are the dead one
traversing between night and day
light and darkness
like a condemned man
unsure of his time
like a drunkard under the spell of wine!
You victim of optical illusion
you live in confusion
and thrive in your own delusion.

Fear of the other world
land of the unknown
bind yourself to the Earth, useless one
for a man afraid to die is a afraid to live
likewise a man afraid yields
to become food for critters

before he is dust
as I shed my material self
with an anti-gravitational thrust.

Whisper

I am alone
on an empty stage
I am alone
in my own rage
I am alone
on my own page
I am alone, in my old age.

Violins

Oh what joy have you found from my harrowing tales?
Of love and tragic kisses from big-chested males...
Love does not leave us covered in scales.
But confines the strong in lock-free cells...
I die a million times for my lover who does not mourn me
I wear my heartache like time until wrinkles adorn me
I seek shelter in a shadow
that instead walks before me
I found my lover in a place unbearable solemn
where tear drops poured forth to sedate me like Valium
I am lost
in a minefield of lies.
An explosion of love
its death in goodbyes.
Left to rot in my lover's excrement
pushed into light from its shadow to bask in sin
comes the bellowing of my tormentors as they sing out
to the mellifluous sound of violins.

Better Company

Don't fucking ask me why I'm bitter
because I hang around like trash and litter
loitering around in your beautiful life
reminding you of a world, much full of strife.
Don't tell me I have reason to be
don't tell me that we're all well and free
Let my blood spill forth onto the street
pour down from my head, onto my feet.
Carry me where
I truly belong, in the cold black dirt.
Home sweet home
Don't tell me I have reason to be,
why don't you just let me free?
For I may go down
go down in vain
and force the world, to feel my pain
let my heartache pour down
like drops of rain
come swooping to the ground, like big white cranes
my world is just a spinning wheel
I'll come around to show you
 how empty I feel
Won't you miss me once I'm gone?
Will you feel, the long, I have longed?
Will you feel the space that used to be?
The empty space, that once was me?
Will you know my lonely hurt?
I'm goin' to home sweet home

into cold black dirt
where I will forever have, what you never gave
laying close to
my neighbor's grave....

Too Dead To Die

I have weathered too many sandstorms
I'm too dried out to cry
I have weathered many sandstorms
and I am too dead to die.
Nothing will fill
my empty heart
nothing will stop
this fade to dark
nothing will change
no matter how I try.
I am too dead
too dead to die.
Nothing will soften
the blows I've encountered
nothing will stop
when nothing matters.
I can write infinitely
of things that do not change
I can go an eternity
and my words will not age.
You may think I am impervious
to wisdom and growth
but I am not impervious
to sleeping in earth.
I can write infinitely
of a world that does not change
as mankind's suffering
continues to rage
I can live a million years
and tell you a million times
I can tell you in different words
in millions of rhymes

and nothing will change
except my lies.
I am too dead
too dead to die.

I Too, Know of Rivers

I too know of rivers
and distant lands,
beyond a stretch,
of Arabian sands,
ancient river
speak to us in tears,
where huts are concrete jungles
and feet become gears.
I too know these rivers
as they course through the lands
like the blood in my veins
and the calluses on my hands
when the diamonds in my ear
turned souls into brands,
I still know these rivers
that rise when I stand...
The spark in my eye
my skin, the color of night
upright in descent
and righteous in flight
I too know these rivers,
muddied and deep
when it whispers in my ear
and lulls me to sleep
a hollow beat
fills my hollowed out heart
knowing the souls of my forefathers
would not want us to part

and the souls of my ancestors
guide us from within
 that the words left on paper
is the blood of my kin.

Chimera of Light

I live my life in darkness
I see the light in vain
I thrive in my own confusion
stifled by my own pain.
Trapped by self-imposed seclusion
illusions,
of a world that does not want me.
Hindered by anxiety.
Rejected by society.
The light is never far
but my journey never ends
a life I live in solitude
a life without many friends.
I reach to the light from darkness
like evil from a crypt
but my foothold is never secure
and neither is my grip.
Never forsake me, Lord
or turn away your ear
and when I talk to you
I pray you that you will hear.
Neither leave me Lord,
don't leave me here to die
without purpose, without meaning
or substance in my life.

Knowing is loving

Someone knows, but does not feel
And holds my heart steady, like beams of steel
My wounds are old, but do not heal
Someone help me, make me feel
I am dying, so young an age
I feel I'm trapped, in an impenetrable cage
A deathblow dealt, from love's piercing blade.
if I could bottle up your love I would
and then I'd throw it
as far as I could
I'd watch it shatter,
into a thousand pieces
then cry my face into a thousand creases.
Thoughts of you run rampant in my brain
when I shatter your delusions
like a speeding freight train.
Someone knows, but does not feel
and holds my heart steady, like beams of steel
my wounds are old, but do not heal
someone help me, make me feel.

Goodbye mommy

I saw the look in your eyes,
for the last time,
knowing inside,
I had to leave you behind,
the look on your face,
was a look of alarm,
when you heard me sobbing ,
when I was pulled from your arms,
and taken away,
wondering will I see you again,
on some other day.
You will ache for my laughter,
and long to wipe my tears,
holding on to my memories,
throughout passing years,
of my life going by,
wishing you could and come see me,
just to say hi,
no one will understand our bond or our pain,
so mommy, goodbye.

My window of hope

I saw the sun shining,
undermining,
the life of an old married witch,
shining down on me,
at the bottom of my ditch.
You were smiling at me on this fine day,
you were smiling at me,
like a sunray,
I saw a window of hope,
on this fine day.
However my hopefulness,
was my blunder,
I failed to see the coming clouds,
I failed to hear the thunder,
I thought that today he would change,
it would be a change from the past,
that is,
until he threw a big rock,
through my window's glass.

Something Wrong?

I live my life
just going along
but I always feel
like something's wrong
something is strange
weird, amiss
odder than a stranger's kiss
I've been lied to
the wool's over my eyes
but we say it's the truth
a thousand times
I feel like the blue skies
are more random lies
and the puffy white clouds
are there as guides
I must float to them
perhaps to address
that the more I learn
the more I know less
and when I'm given compassion
perhaps I've been scorned
and perhaps my death
is when I am born
and when I feel glee
I'm really forlorn
I always feel like something is wrong
And when I'm weak
I'm really strong

and when I'm crying
I'm really in song
and know what I don't
must have known all along
I always feel like something is wrong...

Never Say Goodbye

All I have are memories,
of you my loving friend.
Your tender face,
your warm embrace,
your grace,
is with me until the bitter end.
Hold my heart inside your hand,
because it is filled with so much love,
wipe the tears from my face,
there was no disgrace,
only freedom gifted from heaven above,
I will never say goodbye to you,
it is too much for my heart to bear.
I will never say goodbye to you,
because I will see you when I am there.

Deceitful

My lips have lied a thousand words,
pried from my lips like migrating birds.
To deny my love,
as non-existent,
in my sorrowful soul,
happiness resisted.
The love inside,
smothered unfelt.
Your love is greedy,
and I am wealth.
My lips have kissed misery.
I have embraced my sadness as fantasy.

Rest in Power

For the day and hour is not our choice
I already miss the sound of your voice
Memories that will last us, throughout the years
Your happiness, laughter, and even the tears.
Your comforting words to soothe our fears,
poured like cups of wisdom, to fill our ears.
To see your face and gentle smile,
I'd give anything, to sit and talk for a while.
I'd cherish every word of wisdom and wit,
…and tuck it in my heart so I won't forget.
An encouraging word, or even two,
If you only knew, how much we miss you.
I will search for your smile in the twinkling light
Hear the sound of your music, in the quiet of night
For I know you are with God, shining bright.
I can feel your strength in the passing breeze,
With a moment of sadness, that brings me to my knees.
For God has decided, the day and the hour.
You have lived with strength,
May you rest in power.

Behind every sorrow is a poem.

- E. Hughes

Child of the world
(Written at age 14)

I am a child of the world.
Ridiculed and abused.
I am a child of the world,
unloved and used.
I am child forbidden the luxuries of life.
I am a child of the world,
bruised and cut with a knife
I am a child,
lonely and depressed.
I am a child of the world,
feelings unheard,
and unexpressed.
I am a child,
whose life is unsheltered and cold.
I am an unseen little girl,
whose heart has grown old.
I am an unseen little girl,
whose life is hidden by the shadows of the world.

Beautiful
(Written at age 14)

I hid amongst the bushes,
and showed not,
but an eye.
Ashamed to show my face,
and knew the reason why.
There is a heart and mind inside,
but life is far too cheap.
No one understands the mind,
and that beauty is only skin deep,
I know I am not pretty or beautiful,
and of this I do not weep.
Yet I often feel sick,
of life's cruel trick.
I hid amongst the bushes,
and showed no face,
I know what I am not on the outside, and that I am out of place.
But do not feel gloomy or sad,
and be the sweetest boy or girl,
open your heart to the most wondrous things in life,
and be the most beautiful person in the world.

Never born
(Written at age 16)

I was never,
inside of any woman's womb,
I must have been born,
from some cold tomb,
my heart evaporated,
like a snow flake in June,
as soon as I was old enough,
to watch cartoons.
Wondering why,
I had no mother,
why I never seen,
my baby brother,
now my heart is filled with hate,
because of a system, I could not escape.
Watching my adopted siblings,
 receive their gifts,
playing without sharing,
without any guilt,
wishing that my life, could be rebuilt.
No one ever cared about the mother,
I could not mourn,
it is like I,
 was never born.

Unable to love

I have burned many bridges,
and cast many stones,
even poured vinegar on top,
of my own brittle bones.
Don't extend me your friendship,
it only brings my displeasure,
don't give me your love,
I don't need the pressure,
life has been one rough and bumpy ride,
it is too late for me,
to allow love inside,
all that is left to keep,
is all mine,
I refuse to love,
because of the hard times,
shunning any,
who dare to show me affection,
for fear of experiencing,
anymore rejection,
so I'll forget the past,
without thinking of,
living the rest of my life,
unable to love.

Black Woman Blues

I woke up this morning,
alone in my bed,
wondering if I , were alive or dead,
can't even find, my own house shoes,
I guess it's another day,
of Black woman blues.
In bare feet,
I go downstairs to cook some food,
and get my kids, on' off to school,
my daughter already up,
with her friends outside,
with her hair all' dyed,
and slicked to the side.
My son smells like marijuana, with his eyes
all red,
so I beat his ass
on' out the bed.
I get on' dressed, and go to work,
even though my back, really hurt.
Get my paycheck, and pay my bills,
without money left over, for a thrill.
I come home, feeling the blues,
my kids got their hands out, for $100 shoes,
- they take my cash ,but I give it to em'
just cause they ain't got no dad.
If only I had a strong loving man,
to put a ring on my hand,
and put these kids back in line,

so I can have some free time.
But, I clean my house and go to sleep,
before I cook the kids, some food to eat.
Then I take off my worn out shoes,
ending another day, of Black Woman Blues.
I know I'm not in good health,
but I guess I'm used to doing things,
by myself.
So I'll wake up in the morning,
still feeling used,
to start another day, of
Black Woman Blues.

Just Biding My Time...

Death is freedom from the daily grind
we are wary to leave our children behind
when our bodies die,
what happens to our minds?
Death is freedom from the daily grind.
What happens when we are put to earth
and our bodies return to dust and dirt?
Will God tally up our worth?
Or will we return in another birth?
I look to stars, when they align
hoping for just a little sign...
That death is freedom from the daily grind.
We miss most of our days
working like slaves
building concrete giants
or office-like caves
getting the blues
just watching the news
paying our taxes
and paying our dues
in the end I wonder
what's on the other side
maybe I'll sleep
as I bide my time...
Death is freedom from the daily grind.

I View the World from Swollen Eyes

I watched them sit on the street.
I watched them go without a meal to eat.
I have watched them,
their eyes void of hope,
surviving off scraps most people would consider trash.
We walk past them.
our feet pattering aimlessly over their heads. We spit
and drop our coffee, on the place they call their beds.
What a world, when your human worth is measured
by our most
meaningless material possessions,
Greed, our most evil obsession.
That it is killed or be killed,
eat it all, or starve.
Rather than share, and care.
life isn't, but we make it unfair.
there is more than enough space,
and plenty of air.
Pitter patter aimlessly, but eagerly by,
I watch your determined strides ,
from a place of broken dreams, where only pigeons
dare fly,
beneath grey skies,
as a coin plops into my cup,
I watch your determined strides,
I view it all absently from swollen eyes.

Love. Hope.

Be Innocent, Little One

Go to bed,
sleepy head,
try not to look,
as if you're dead,
don't wake up,
from beautiful dreams,
to a world of horror,
filled with screams,
dance to music,
soft and sweet,
close your ears,
to lies and deceit,
heaven awaits all that is good,
so try to do the things you should,
for you little one,
a tender kiss,
and may heaven grant your,
every wish.

Where I Want To Be

Lift your eyes to heaven,
where everyone longs to be,
lift your eyes to heaven,
where everyone is free.
It is bigger than this whole wide world,
and bluer than any sea,
lift your eyes to heaven,
that's where I want to be.
This is where dreamers dream of being,
lift your eyes to heaven and sing,
every man in harmony,
without discord,
leave our troubles to the world,
glimmers of sunshine
twinkling light,
imagine a quiet and peaceful night,
splashes of color shining bright.
Lift your eyes to heaven,
that's where I want to be,
lift your eyes to heaven,
and sing when you are free.

Moonstars
(Written at age 19)

My pillow is much like a tombstone.
I lie in a grave of dreams,
don't wake me when I am sleeping,
to put me out of misery.
My heart the bleeding organ,
pierced by a dagger of inspiration,
blinding like the sun,
I remain as subtle as the moon

Listen

Will you listen to me
when I talk?
and do not stare,
or even gawk?
Will you listen to me
and find no fault?
In the way I stand
or even walk?
When I hold my shoulders square?
Do you promise not to be unfair?
Do you promise,
not to laugh?
Or snicker if I make a gaffe?
Will you listen
When I speak?
Nor bully me when I am meek?
Or raise your eyebrows,
when I'm tongue in cheek?
Will you listen, when I speak?

Sunrays

I was born,
a tiny wonder,
with beautiful dreams,
when wake and in slumber,
praise be,
May I learn from life's hard lessons,
and appreciate,
every little blessing,
dear Lord bless me with hope and compassion,
and love that will live in me for the rest of my days,
that shines from my heart,
like beams of SUNRAYS...

My Arrival

It is time for me to open my eyes
I dare not sleep on my dreams
I don't have time for tear drops
to pour down into the stream.
It is time for me to heal
heal without delay
time that I work hard
kneel, for I must pray.
Venting my desires
for my own survival
call it whatever you may
I call it my arrival.
It is time for me to sleep.
Sleep for I must rest
to free myself of burdens
that lay upon my breast.
If it died you may call it a revival.
But it is detrimental to my survival
call it whatever you may,
I call it my arrival.

Loving Way

I want to share your loving way,
we can stay in bed,
until midday,
close the curtains,
pull down the shades,
cool our bodies,
drink lemonade,
I long to feel your loving way,
we can stay nude while at play,
call in to work,
on the next day...
unplug the phone and hide,
sharing our love...
staying inside.

Make Love to Me

Make it gentle,
make it sweet,
make it simple,
Make love to me.
Lay upon my skin,
like bark upon a tree,
make it tender,
Make love to me.
Let us connect,
spiritually,
respectfully,
Make love to me.
Not a conquest,
don't call it sex,
caress my neck,
Make love to me.
Like each snowflake,
may our encounters be unique,
for heaven's sake,
we've love to make,
so make love to me!
Especially,
love me ever,
so carefully.
Emotionally,
bittersweet,
hold my hand,

kiss my cheek,
hold me tightly,
make love to me.

Come My Love

Come my love,
fill me up
overflowing
in my cup
I carry you
deep within
and even touch
your beautiful skin
I watch you closely
eyes aglow
you cover me
like a blanket of snow
I carry you
within my soul
desire burning
like red-hot coal.

Friend

I am blessed,
I am loved,
thanks to you dear Lord,
I am not alone.
A trusted friend,
who loves so much,
everything is light,
in sight of your touch.
Every breeze,
every stream,
every leaf,
from every tree,
a sturdy bridge from earth to heaven's gate,
a shoulder to cry on when I need escape,
I am blessed to have a friend in you,
I am blessed to have a friend like you.

True Happiness

My days of crying have come to an end
The time for my life has just began
No more loneliness
No more stress
No more days of being depressed
Yes!
My life is no longer a mess
And each day I live is one big fest.
No more strangers in my reflection
And my whole life is pure perfection
making the best decisions from every selection.
Yes I am who I am,
not who others want me to be
and I've found true happiness inside of me.
No more quests for love from others you see,
I've found true happiness inside of me!
No more scrambling around for the scraps somebody
left,
I've learned to love my own true self,
Yes I am who I am and not who *YOU* want me to be,
and I've found true happiness, inside of me.

About the Author

E. Hughes is a novelist and writer of more than twenty-five years and has over twenty published books in multiple genres from fiction novels, nonfiction works, poetry, and children's books to date. Her first book of poetry, "*Beyond the Plain*" was published in 2003 with a second edition in 2018. Her second collection of poetry, "*Digital Smiles*" was released in 2024, with her collection of unreleased poetry in *Space, Time, and Loneliness*, released shortly after. Hughes is also the author of *Time and the Multi-Universe: a philosophy of time and time travel*, *Reality Unbound: The Digital Mind (and the nature of reality)* and the novel, *Sixth Iteration*.

www.ingramcontent.com/pod-product-compliance
Lightning Source LLC
Chambersburg PA
CBHW020623300426
44113CB00007B/759